To my brother Paco,

Your unwavering belief in the existence of something greater is now being affirmed by the advancements in AI, guiding our journeys as you boldly dream of venturing "where no man has gone before."

Love

Sister

"Humans the New Dinasaur?" Is AI Taking over earth?

Chapter 1: Introduction

Title: Rise of the Robot Overlords... or Just Overblown Hype?

Section 1: The Age of AI: From Sci-Fi to Everyday Reality

Step 1: Dive into the wild world of AI

Let's embark on a journey through the fascinating realm of AI, where what was once confined to the pages of science fiction novels has now become an integral part of our daily lives. From the rudimentary chatbots of yesteryears to the sophisticated virtual assistants like Siri and Alexa that we rely on for everything from weather updates to recipe suggestions, the evolution of AI has been nothing short of extraordinary. Imagine if George Jetson's Rosie had a software upgrade and could now manage your entire household with just a few voice commands!

Step 2: Tackle the big question that's been keeping us all up at night

Now, let's address the elephant in the room—or should I say, the robot in the room? The question on everyone's minds: are we hurtling towards a dystopian future where AI reigns supreme, or is the fear of AI taking over just a tad overblown? It's natural to have concerns about the rapid advancement of technology, but let's take a moment to separate fact from fiction and explore some common fears surrounding AI.

One prevalent fear is that AI will lead to widespread job loss as machines take over tasks traditionally performed by humans. However, history has shown us that while technology may eliminate certain jobs, it also creates new opportunities and industries. For example, the rise of the automobile may have spelled the end for horse-drawn carriage drivers, but it also gave birth to the automotive industry, creating millions of new jobs in the process.

Another concern is the idea of AI becoming too intelligent and surpassing human capabilities, leading to a scenario straight out of a sci-fi thriller where machines rebel against their creators. While it's true that AI has the potential to become incredibly powerful, it's important to remember that it's ultimately humans who control the development and deployment of AI systems. We're more likely to see AI being used to augment human intelligence rather than replace it entirely—think Iron Man with his trusty AI assistant, J.A.R.V.I.S., rather than the Terminator.

Chapter 2: The Age of AI: Understanding the Landscape

Title: AI for Dummies (And Everyone Else)

Section 1: The AI Crash Course: From Chatbots to Cybernetic Overlords

We're taking a crash course in all things AI, explaining concepts like machine learning and neural networks in a way that even your cat could understand. From productivity hacks to robo-pizza delivery, we'll explore how AI is revolutionizing industries and everyday life with wit and humor. Remember when we thought the future would be full of flying cars and robot maids? Well, the future is here, and it's more like having a really smart but slightly annoying friend who always has the answer but won't stop correcting your grammar.

Section 2: AI: The Good, the Bad, and the Self-Driving Ugly

From self-driving cars to AI-generated art, we'll explore the wild and wonderful world of AI applications. But it's not all sunshine and rainbows—we'll also discuss the potential downsides, from privacy concerns to job displacement. After all, who needs a robot to write poetry when you've got a human with a really good rhyming dictionary? And let's not forget the joy of having a virtual assistant who's always ready to answer your burning questions... even if you didn't actually ask.

Section 3: The Future is Bright: How AI is Fueling Innovation

We'll peer into the crystal ball and ponder what the future holds for AI, from autonomous drones to AI-generated art. But fear not, dear reader, for in the pages ahead, we'll confront these fears with humor, insight, and maybe just a hint of existential dread. After all, if there's one thing humans excel at, it's finding creative ways to avoid being replaced by our robot overlords... at least for now.

Chapter 3: Benefits of AI Adoption

Title: AI: Making Life Easier... Unless You're a Terminator

Section 1: The AI Advantage: From Productivity Hacks to Robo-Pizza Delivery

Step 1: Dive into the ways AI is making life easier

Let's delve into the myriad ways in which AI is revolutionizing our daily lives, transforming mundane tasks into seamless experiences and paving the way for a future straight out of our wildest sci-fi fantasies. Picture this: you wake up to the gentle hum of your AI-powered alarm clock, which not only knows your preferred wake-up time but also adjusts the lighting and temperature in your room to match your circadian rhythm. As you stumble into the kitchen, still half-asleep, your coffee maker —equipped with AI technology—has already brewed the perfect cup of joe, customized to your exact specifications.

Step 2: Tackle the potential downsides of AI adoption

But amidst the convenience and efficiency that AI brings, there are valid concerns that warrant attention. One such concern is the fear of job displacement as automation becomes more prevalent across various industries. However, it's important to recognize that while AI may indeed automate certain tasks, it also creates new job opportunities in emerging fields such as dat a science, machine learning engineering, and AI ethics.

Additionally, there's the issue of data privacy and security in an increasingly interconnected world where AI systems collect vast amounts of personal information. While AI has the potential to revolutionize industries like healthcare by analyzing patient data to improve diagnoses and treatments, it also raises questions about who owns and controls this sensitive data. Striking the right balance between innovation and protection of individual privacy rights is crucial as we navigate the AI-driven future.

Chapter 4: The Changing Nature of Work

Title: Will Work for Bytes: Surviving the Robot Apocalypse

Section 1: The Rise of the Machines: How AI is Reshaping the Job Market

Step 1: Dive into the impact of AI on the job market

Let's explore how the proliferation of AI technologies is reshaping the landscape of employment, sparking debates about the future of work and the role of humans in an increasingly automated world. Picture this: you're sitting at your desk, scrolling through job listings on your AI-powered job search platform, when you come across an intriguing opportunity. The job description sounds perfect—until you notice the dreaded line: "experience with AI and machine learning algorithms preferred." Suddenly, you find yourself grappling with the realization that your dream job may require skills you never even knew existed.

Step 2: Tackle the fear of job displacement

But amidst the uncertainty and anxiety surrounding AI's impact on employment, it's important to separate fact from fiction and address common misconceptions. While it's true that AI and automation may eliminate certain jobs, they also create new opportunities and demand for skills in fields such as data analysis, cybersecurity, and human-AI collaboration. Rather than viewing AI as a threat to job security, we should embrace it as a catalyst for innovation and career advancement.

Chapter 5: Human vs. Machine: The Skills Debate

Title: Are We Doomed to Become the World's Most Overqualified Paperweights?

Section 1: The Skills Gap: Fact or Fiction?

Step 1: Dive into the discussion on the skills gap

Let's dive into the ongoing debate surrounding the so-called "skills gap" in the age of AI, where rapid technological advancements are reshaping the requirements for success in the workforce. Picture this: you're attending a career fair, surrounded by eager job seekers armed with resumes and LinkedIn profiles showcasing their impressive qualifications. But as you glance around the room, you can't help but wonder if your own skill set is becoming increasingly obsolete in the face of AI and automation.

Step 2: Tackle the fear of skill obsolescence

But before succumbing to despair, let's challenge the notion that humans are destined to become obsolete in the age of AI. While it's true that AI has the potential to automate routine tasks, it also amplifies the value of uniquely human skills such as creativity, emotional intelligence, and critical thinking. Rather than viewing AI as a threat to our livelihoods, we should embrace it as a catalyst for personal and professional growth, seizing opportunities to upskill and adapt to the changing demands of the digital economy.

Chapter 6: The Rise of Passive Income and Wealth Disparity

Title: From Rags to Riches... to Even Richer Robots

Section 1: The Age of Automation: How AI is Creating a Wealth Divide

Step 1: Dive into the phenomenon of passive income and wealth disparity

Let's explore the double-edged sword of AI-driven automation, where the promise of passive income coexists with widening wealth disparities and socioeconomic inequalities. Picture this: you're scrolling through your social media feed, bombarded by ads promising untold riches through passive income streams like affiliate marketing, dropshipping, and cryptocurrency trading. But as you ponder the allure of financial independence, you can't help but wonder if these opportunities are accessible to everyone—or if they merely perpetuate existing disparities in wealth and privilege.

Step 2: Tackle the implications of wealth inequality

But amidst the allure of passive income and the tantalizing promise of financial freedom, it's essential to confront the harsh reality of widening wealth gaps and socioeconomic disparities. While AI-driven automation has the potential to generate unprecedented prosperity, it also exacerbates inequalities by concentrating wealth and power in the hands of a privileged few. As we navigate the complexities of the digital economy, it's imperative to address structural inequities and implement policies that promote inclusive growth and shared prosperity for all.

Chapter 7: The Future of Humanity in an AI World

Title: Welcome to Tomorrowland: Population - Humans, Robots, and the Occasional Cyborg

Section 1: The Brave New World of AI: What Lies Ahead?

Step 1: Dive into the possibilities of an AI-dominated future

Let's peer into the crystal ball and ponder what the future holds for humanity in a world where AI reigns

supreme, reshaping our societies, economies, and even our very notion of what it means to be human. Picture this: you're strolling through a bustling cityscape, surrounded by self-driving cars, delivery drones, and humanoid robots performing tasks once reserved for human hands. As you marvel at the dizzying pace of technological progress, you can't help but wonder what lies ahead for our species in this brave new world of AI.

Step 2: Tackle the existential questions surrounding AI

But amidst the awe and wonder of technological innovation, it's essential to confront the existential questions and ethical dilemmas that accompany the rise of AI. From concerns about job displacement and algorithmic bias to fears of AI surpassing human intelligence and autonomy, the future of humanity in an AI-dominated world raises profound and complex challenges. As we navigate this uncertain terrain, it's crucial to uphold our values, safeguard our humanity, and chart a course towards a future where humans and machines coexist harmoniously, enriching each other's lives in ways we've yet to imagine.

Chapter 8: Who's Training Who?

Title: AI and Humans: Partners in Progress or Competitors in Evolution?

Section 1: The Symbiotic Relationship Between AI and Humans

Step 1: Dive into the question of AI's dependence on humans

Let's delve into the intriguing question at the heart of the AI-human relationship: does artificial intelligence truly need humans to function, or is it capable of autonomous operation? Picture this: you're marveling at the astounding capabilities of a state-of-the-art AI system, capable of processing vast amounts of data and making complex decisions in milliseconds. But as you peel back the layers of its intelligence, you realize that behind every algorithm and neural network lies a human creator who imbued it with knowledge, logic, and purpose.

Step 2: Tackle the complexities of AI's autonomy

As we contemplate the extent of AI's dependence on human guidance and expertise, it becomes evident that while AI can indeed operate autonomously to a certain extent, its true potential is unlocked through human intervention and supervision. While AI systems excel at

processing data and executing tasks with precision, they lack the creativity, intuition, and moral judgment that define the human experience. In essence, AI serves as a tool—a powerful one, no doubt—but ultimately, it is humans who imbue it with meaning and direction.

Step 3: Explore the symbiosis of AI and human intelligence

But amidst the discussion of AI's dependence on humans, it's crucial to recognize the reciprocal nature of the relationship.

Just as AI relies on human creators to design and train its algorithms, humans benefit from AI's computational power and analytical capabilities to augment their own intelligence and productivity. Together, humans and AI form a symbiotic partnership, each leveraging the strengths of the other to achieve feats that neither could accomplish alone. As we navigate this evolving relationship, it's essential to strike a balance between harnessing the potential of AI and preserving the unique qualities that make us human.

Step 1: Dive into the question of AI's dependence on humans

Let's delve into the intriguing question at the heart of the AI-human relationship: does artificial intelligence truly need humans to function, or is it capable of autonomous operation? Picture this: you're marveling at the astounding capabilities of a state-of-the-art AI system, capable of processing vast amounts of data and making complex decisions in milliseconds. But as you peel back the layers of its intelligence, you realize that behind every algorithm and neural network lies a human creator who imbued it with knowledge, logic, and purpose. In this symbiotic dance between human ingenuity and machine learning, it becomes evident that while AI can indeed operate

autonomously to a certain extent, its true potential is unlocked through human intervention and supervision.

In conclusion, the journey through the intertwined worlds of humans and artificial intelligence has illuminated the complexities and nuances of our evolving relationship with technology. From the dawn of AI to the uncertainties of its future impact, we've explored the symbiotic partnership between human ingenuity and machine learning, recognizing that while AI may possess remarkable capabilities, it ultimately relies on human guidance and creativity to fulfill its potential. As we navigate the opportunities and challenges of the AI-driven future, let us embrace the possibilities of collaboration and innovation, leveraging the strengths of both humans and machines to shape a world where technology serves as a catalyst for progress and human flourishing. With humor, insight, and a touch of imagination, we've embarked on a journey through the brave new world of AI, where the boundaries between science fiction and reality blur, and the possibilities are limited only by our imagination.

In closing, "Humans the New Dinosaurs? Is AI taking over?" serves as a captivating exploration of the evolving relationship between humanity and artificial intelligence. From delving into the depths of AI's capabilities to addressing the fears and uncertainties surrounding its rise, each chapter has provided insights into the symbiotic partnership between humans and machines. We've journeyed through the wild world of AI, dissecting common fears and misconceptions, and uncovering the truth behind the hype. Along the way, we've laughed at the absurdities of AI billionaires and pondered the existential questions of our technological future.

Through it all, one question has remained at the forefront: Who's Training Who? As we've peeled back the layers of AI's intelligence, we've discovered that while it possesses remarkable capabilities, it ultimately relies on human ingenuity and guidance to reach its full potential. Just as AI augments human intelligence and productivity, humans imbue AI with meaning, direction, and purpose. In this symbiotic relationship, each entity complements the other, forming a partnership that propels us towards a future where technology serves as a tool for progress rather than a threat to our existence.

As we navigate the complexities of the AI-driven world, let us embrace the possibilities of collaboration and innovation, leveraging the strengths of both humans and machines to shape a future that benefits all. By addressing the challenges of AI integration with humor, insight, and a touch of imagination, we can ensure that the answer to the question "Humans the New Dinosaurs? Is AI taking over?" is one of hope, resilience, and boundless potential.

In wrapping up our wild ride through the world of AI, let's take a moment to chuckle at the cosmic joke that is "Humans the New Dinosaurs? Is AI taking over?" Sure, the title sounds like the setup for a sci-fi comedy, but hey, truth is often stranger than fiction!

As we've journeyed through the labyrinth of AI's capabilities and pondered the existential questions of our technological future, one thing has become abundantly clear: we're in this together, humans and machines, like an odd couple in a buddy cop movie. While AI may be the flashy new recruit with all the latest gadgets, it still needs us old-timers to show it the ropes and keep it from causing too much mischief. After all, who else is going to remind it to say "please" and "thank you"?

So, as we peel back the layers of AI's intelligence like a particularly stubborn onion, let's find solace in the absurdity of it all and take comfort in the knowledge that, despite the

uncertainties of the future, we're in good company. With humor as our guide and curiosity as our compass, we'll navigate the twists and turns of the AI-driven world with a sense of peace, knowing that no matter how advanced the technology may become, there will always be room for a good old-fashioned human touch.

As we bid farewell to our journey through the brave new world of AI, let's raise a toast to the partnership between humans and machines, to the laughter shared along the way, and to the endless possibilities that lie ahead. After all, in a world where even the most sophisticated AI can't tell a joke quite like we can, there's no need to fear the future—because as long as there are humans around, there will always be plenty of laughs to go around. Cheers to that!